W9-BJC-272

THIS LAND CALLED AMERICA: **CONNECTICUT**

CREATIVE EDUCATION

Published by Creative Education
P.O. Box 227, Mankato, Minnesota 56002
Creative Education is an imprint of The Creative Company
www.thecreativecompany.us

Book and cover design by Blue Design (www.bluedes.com)
Art direction by Rita Marshall
Printed in the United States of America

Photographs by Alamy (North Wind Picture Archives), Corbis
(Bettmann, Mark E. Gibson, Robert Holmes, James Marshall, Gabe
Palmer, Phil Schermeister, Tim Wright), Getty Images (Jose Azel, Glenn
Beanland, Gary Buss, John T. Carbone, Mitch Epstein, Lionel Green/
Hulton Archive, Hulton Archive, Michael Ochs Archives, MPI, Phil
Nelson, Chris Niedenthal//Time Life Pictures, Stock Montage)

Copyright © 2009 Creative Education
International copyright reserved in all countries. No part of this book
may be reproduced in any form without written permission from the
publisher.

Library of Congress Cataloging-in-Publication Data
Labairon, Cassandra Sharri.
Connecticut / by Cassandra Labairon.
p. cm. — (This land called America)
Includes bibliographical references and index.
ISBN 978-1-58341-632-7
1. Connecticut—Juvenile literature. I. Title. II. Series.
F94.3.L33 2008
974.6—dc22          2007015002

First Edition
9 8 7 6 5 4 3 2 1

This Land Called America

# CONNECTICUT

Cassandra Labairon

# Connecticut

CASSANDRA LABAIRON

THE WATERS OF NEW ENGLAND'S LARGEST RIVER, THE CONNECTICUT, RISE AND FALL WITH THE OCEAN TIDES. IN THE DEPTHS OF THE RIVER, SCUBA DIVERS SEARCH FOR CREATURES SUCH AS MUSSELS AND MUDPUPPIES. ON THE SURFACE OF THE WATER, PEOPLE ENJOY TAKING HISTORIC RIVERBOAT RIDES, EXPERIENCING THE SCENIC RIVER THE WAY PEOPLE DID MORE THAN 100 YEARS AGO. AS THE TOURISTS FLOAT DOWNSTREAM FOR AN HOUR, THEY SPY LOONS AND OSPREY NEAR THE SHORE AND BALD EAGLES FLYING OVERHEAD. IN THE CONNECTICUT RIVER VALLEY, AS IN ALL PARTS OF THIS SMALL EASTERN STATE, PEOPLE DO NOT HAVE TO GO FAR TO EXPERIENCE THE NATURAL WONDERS OF CONNECTICUT.

YEAR
1614 Fur trader Adriaen Block navigates the Connecticut River for the Dutch.
EVENT

# The New World

A number of American Indian tribes lived on the land now called Connecticut when explorers from Europe arrived in the 1600s. The Pequot, Mohegan, and Quiripi were some of the peoples who called the forests, valleys, and beaches of the area home. In the early 1600s, Dutch navigator and

fur trader Adriaen Block traveled along the East Coast to set up a fur trade with the native tribes. Block discovered the Connecticut River in 1614, but he did not stay in Connecticut for long.

In 1636, English people settled the Connecticut Colony. They were attracted to the area because of its rich farmland. They also wanted a place where they could practice their religion freely. These early colonists were strict Puritans who wanted to focus their lives on serving God.

At first, relations between the colonists and the area's tribes were peaceful. The tribes helped the colonists survive

*People from Massachusetts traveled through peaceful countryside (above) and winter storms (opposite) to settle early towns in Connecticut.*

YEAR

1637    The Pequot War breaks out, and the English colonists conquer the Pequot tribe.

EVENT

- 7 -

State bird: American robin

in the new land. However, as time went on, problems began to develop.

The Pequot tribe was the largest and most powerful group in the region. Conflicts between colonists and the Pequot peaked in 1637, when the colonists fought against the tribe in the Pequot War. Hundreds of Pequots were killed, and captured survivors were sold into slavery.

Before the United States became a country, Connecticut had the first written constitution in America. Political leaders John Haynes and Roger Ludlow, along with minister Thomas Hooker, wrote the Fundamental Orders of Connecticut. The Fundamental Orders were adopted January 14, 1639, and Haynes was named territorial governor.

Even though Connecticut had its own governor, it was still ruled by England. By 1660, many colonists disagreed with England's rule, so Governor John Winthrop went to England to discuss their concerns with King Charles II. Winthrop came home with a royal charter explaining the colonists' rights with the king's approval. In 1687, though, England wanted to take the charter back. A colonist hid the charter in a hollow spot in a large white oak tree. The tree became known as the "Charter Oak," and its species is now the state tree.

America's war for independence from England began

*The great-great-great-grandson of Governor John Winthrop was a famous mathematician (opposite).*

YEAR

1764 The first issue of the *Connecticut Courant*, the oldest American newspaper in continuous existence, is printed.

EVENT

- 9 -

*Nathan Hale (far right) was a schoolteacher before he enlisted as a soldier in 1775.*

*Unemployed people all over the U.S. stood in long lines looking for jobs during the Great Depression.*

in 1775. The Declaration of Independence was signed a year later. Nathan Hale, a young soldier from Connecticut who was captured by the British, famously said, "I only regret that I have but one life to lose for my country." The British surrendered at Yorktown, Virginia, on October 19, 1781, and the new U.S. Congress officially declared the war over in 1783.

Connecticut became a state January 9, 1788. It was the fifth state admitted to the union and the fifth to ratify, or agree to, the U.S. Constitution. Throughout the 1800s and into the early 1900s, Connecticut became known for its manufacturing industries. Factories for ship building and textile production opened. The state changed dramatically. People moved from farms into the cities. New immigrants from Europe were also drawn to the state's urban areas because of the jobs created by the factories.

Those jobs were in short supply during the Great Depression of the 1930s, though. People in Connecticut lost money and jobs during that decade after the U.S. stock market crashed. But the state quickly recovered during World War II, using its ship-building factories to make submarines and aircraft for the war.

YEAR
**1774** Three representatives from Connecticut attend the First Continental Congress to help establish colonists' rights.
EVENT

# A Little Bit of Everything

LOCATED IN THE NORTHEASTERN U.S., CONNECTICUT IS THE THIRD-SMALLEST STATE IN THE COUNTRY. ONLY RHODE ISLAND AND DELAWARE HAVE LESS LAND AREA. CONNECTICUT IS BORDERED BY NEW YORK TO THE WEST, RHODE ISLAND TO THE EAST, MASSACHUSETTS TO THE NORTH, AND LONG ISLAND SOUND TO THE SOUTH.

Although Connecticut is a small state, it has a variety of landscapes and wildlife. Fox, deer, coyote, and rabbits live in its forests. The Atlantic Ocean and local rivers and lakes are home to both freshwater and saltwater fish. Both forests and water also attract a wide range of birds, from owls and warblers to geese and sandpipers.

The state receives a portion of its income from farm products such as eggs, apples, vegetables, and tobacco. Connecticut broadleaf tobacco has been one of the most sought-after varieties of tobacco for making cigars since the 1830s.

Connecticut is typically divided into four geographic regions. The Western New England Upland covers the western part of the state. The Connecticut Valley Lowland sits in the center, and the Eastern New England Upland region lies in the east. The three sections are connected in the southern part of the state by the Coastal Lowlands, a narrow strip of land that runs along Long Island Sound.

The Western New England Upland is mountainous and forested. In the Taconic Mountains, Connecticut's highest point, Mt. Frissel, looms 2,380 feet (725 m) in the air. The state's largest lake, Candlewood Lake, is also found in this area. The Housatonic River flows north and south through the entire region.

*Connecticut's many harbors are home to sailing and fishing boats (opposite). Those who would rather not get wet can hike in the Western New England Upland (above).*

YEAR
1776  Connecticut's four representatives sign the Declaration of Independence.
EVENT

- 13 -

The Connecticut Valley Lowland is a 20-mile (32 km) wide area in the center of the state. The Lowland surrounds the Connecticut River, which divides the state in half. The American Indian word *Quinnehtukqut*, from which early Americans took the name for the state, means "place of the long river." The best farmland is found in the Lowland, and so is Hartford, the state capital.

The Eastern New England Upland includes narrow river valleys and low hills. It is heavily forested. The state's lowest point is found where Connecticut's land meets the Long Island Sound at the state's southern border.

*Forests of tall trees (opposite) line the edges of Connecticut's namesake river, the Connecticut River (above), which offers smooth sailing for small boats.*

1848    Slavery is abolished in Connecticut.

The low-lying, flat region that borders Long Island Sound is known as the Coastal Lowlands. Several important harbors are found along the coast. Because the harbors are readily accessible to ships and allow for easy movement of goods, they have been vital to the development of the state's economy.

Three of Connecticut's most important cities—Bridgeport, New London, and New Haven—are located along Long Island Sound. The Sound has become polluted by industrial waste from the cities' factories over the years, and Connecticut, like many states, is now putting into place more earth-friendly policies to help preserve it.

*Connecticut's 250-mile (402 km) shoreline extends from such towns as Greenwich to Stonington.*

Connecticut's climate is generally mild, but temperatures can be much colder in the mountains and much warmer in the central part of the state. In January, the average temperature is 27 °F (-2.8 °C), while June's average is 70 °F (21 °C). Average precipitation statewide is 46 inches (117 cm) per year. Connecticut's most threatening weather is a coastal storm, or "nor'easter." These storms are capable of producing strong winds and heavy rainfall. They generate the greatest snowstorms in the winter months, contributing to the 25 inches (64 cm) of snow that usually fall on Connecticut.

YEAR
1877
EVENT

The world's first telephone exchange, or switchboard, is opened in New Haven.

# The Nutmeggers

THE NATIVE TRIBES THAT LIVED IN CONNECTICUT BEFORE THE COLONISTS ARRIVED WERE FARMERS. THEY RAISED CORN, BEANS, SQUASH, AND TOBACCO. AFTER THE ENGLISH COLONISTS BEGAN ARRIVING IN THE 1600S, SOME OF THE TRIBES BANDED TOGETHER. ONE OF THE LARGEST GROUPS WAS THE PEQUOT. THEY TRAVELED THROUGH RIVERS IN CANOES MADE BY FELLING AND

ARTIST: F. O. C. DARLEY.

*American Indians in Connecticut hunted wild animals in addition to raising crops.*

hollowing out large trees. They lived in semi-permanent villages so that they could be ready to move to different places when the seasons changed.

Both men and women of the Pequot tribe created artwork, made music, and practiced medicine. They were known for their storytelling, beadwork, and baskets. Children did many chores. But they also played ball games, played with cornhusk dolls, or practiced shooting with bows and arrows.

*After many years of peace, war broke out between the Pequots and the settlers in 1637.*

The first colonists in Connecticut were from other New England states and Great Britain. In the middle of the 19th century, there was a famine in Ireland. Thousands of people

*Noah Webster's (opposite) dictionary reflected the way 19th-century Americans used the English language.*

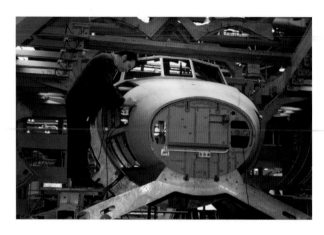

*Companies based in Connecticut cities such as Plainville and Middletown make parts for aircraft.*

died from hunger, and thousands more sailed to the U.S. They settled in eastern states such as Connecticut.

From the mid-1800s through the mid-1900s, Italians, Germans, Greeks, Poles, and other Europeans also immigrated to work in Connecticut's new factories. In the last half of the 20th century, the ethnic background of Connecticut's citizens changed once again. African Americans, Puerto Ricans, Chinese, and Russians added to the diversity of the state.

Most of Connecticut's wealth comes from industry. Many companies based in Connecticut produce engines for aircraft. The state is also a leader in electronics, machinery, and computer equipment.

Connecticut residents are known as "Nutmeggers." The exact origin of the nickname is uncertain, but some believe it comes from the time when peddlers, or traveling salesmen, sold goods door-to-door. These peddlers sold exotic spices such as nutmeg and sometimes tricked people into buying fake nutmeg.

Noah Webster was a famous Nutmegger. He was born in Hartford in 1758. When Webster was 43, he started

YEAR
1897   The Pope Manufacturing Company of Hartford begins making automobiles.
EVENT

YEAR

1907   The first Boy Scout Troop in Connecticut (Troop 1) is established in East Hartford.

EVENT

*Although Harriet Beecher Stowe was born and died in Connecticut, she spent much of her adult life in Ohio.*

writing the first American dictionary. It took him more than 27 years to write the 70,000-word dictionary. He finally finished it in 1828 at the age of 70. Webster's book taught children how to read, spell, and pronounce words. It was the most popular American book of its time. When Noah Webster died in 1843, he was considered an American hero.

*Stowe published UNCLE TOM'S CABIN in 1852, and by 1859, the book had sold almost 300,000 copies.*

Another American hero was Harriet Beecher Stowe. She was born in 1811 in Litchfield, Connecticut. She is best known as the author of *Uncle Tom's Cabin,* a story about a slave's escape from the American South to safety in the North. It helped the anti-slavery cause and contributed to the start of the Civil War. Stowe was popular because her works dealt with issues of her time, such as slavery, women's rights, and the rise of industry. She earned a place in the National Women's Hall of Fame in 1986.

YEAR

1911    The Connecticut College for Women is founded in New London.

EVENT

- 23 -

Katharine Hepburn in 1938

Academy Award-winning actress Katharine Hepburn staged her first play when she was eight years old. In 1915, the budding actress put on fellow Connecticut native Harriet Beecher Stowe's *Uncle Tom's Cabin* for her family and friends in a backyard theater. The Hartford native went on to become one of Hollywood's best-known and loved actresses, starring in movies such as *Guess Who's Coming to Dinner* and *On Golden Pond*.

*Katharine Hepburn, who grew up near author Mark Twain's home (opposite) in Hartford, starred in movies with other famous actors of the day such as Cary Grant (above).*

YEAR

1960    Ground is broken for the first building in Hartford's Constitution plaza.

# Eyes on the Future

STATE PARKS AND FORESTS ARE FOUND IN EVERY REGION
OF CONNECTICUT. EACH PARK OFFERS ITS OWN
ATTRACTIONS. PARKS CAN BE FOUND IN THE MOUNTAINS,
FORESTS, RIVER VALLEYS, AND ALONG CONNECTICUT'S
250-MILE (402 KM) SHORELINE. AT BLUFF POINT
COASTAL RESERVE, FOR INSTANCE, PEOPLE CAN EXPLORE
PART OF LONG ISLAND SOUND ON MOUNTAIN BIKES OR

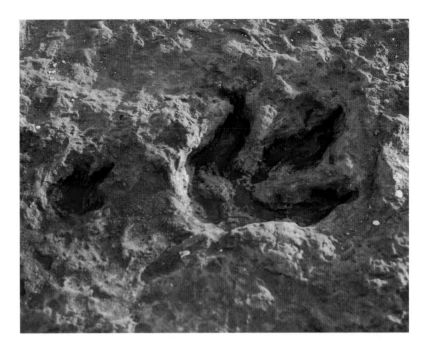

*The fossilized footprints of dinosaurs are protected by a giant dome at the popular Dinosaur State Park.*

horseback. The parks offer numerous opportunities for outdoor activities such as camping, hiking, fishing, boating, and swimming.

One of the most intriguing parks is Dinosaur State Park. It has fossil tracks that were made 200 million years ago. Located in Rocky Hill, the park is one of the largest dinosaur track sites in the world. The park also has plant life that is much like that which was around when the dinosaurs lived, making it a popular destination for dinosaur enthusiasts.

Outdoor enthusiasts also take advantage of Connecticut's section of the Appalachian Trail. Many hikers from around the world trek along the Appalachian Trail. Completed in 1937, the path goes through 14 states and is more than 2,000 miles (3,219 km) long. Fifty-two miles (84 km) of the trail go through Connecticut. Most of it follows along the ridge of the Housatonic River Valley in the northwestern corner of the state.

*Visitors enjoy traveling through the Connecticut woods in the fall when the leaves change color.*

Connecticut attracts tourists who enjoy history and culture. In restored colonial villages, visitors can get a glimpse of what life was like for the American Indians and early settlers. Connecticut is home to several nationally celebrated muse-

*The village of Mystic Seaport is a living history museum of 19th-century shipping and sailing.*

ums and art galleries. There are more than 40 museums in Connecticut. Bridgeport's Barnum Museum, which opened in 1893, features an exhibit dedicated to the life of P. T. Barnum. Born in Bethel, Connecticut, Barnum rose to fame through his career as a circus showman.

New Haven, Connecticut, is home to Yale University. Yale is the third-oldest university in the U.S. It was founded in 1701. It is one of eight Ivy League schools, which are considered some of the top colleges in the country. The university has educated many political leaders, including American presidents such as Gerald Ford, George H. W. Bush, and Bill Clinton.

From 1979 to 1997, the Hartford Whalers of the National Hockey League called Connecticut home. Since the Whalers moved to North Carolina and became the Carolina Hurricanes in 1997, Connecticut has been without any professional sports teams. To make up for the Whalers' loss, Hartford

YEAR

1974     Ella Grasso becomes the first woman elected as governor of Connecticut.

EVENT

Connecticut's grand
state capitol, located in
Hartford, has been in
use since its completion
in 1879.

| YEAR | |
|---|---|
| 1982 | Dr. Robert K. Jarvik, a Stamford native, invents the world's first artificial heart. |
| EVENT | |

# QUICK FACTS

Population: 3,504,809

Largest city: Bridgeport (pop. 139,664)

Capital: Hartford

Entered the union: January 9, 1788

Nicknames: Constitution State, Nutmeg State

State flower: mountain laurel

State bird: American robin

Size: 5,543 sq mi (14,356 sq km)—48th-biggest in U.S.

Major industries: manufacturing, finance, real estate, farming

established a new team in the American Hockey League, the Hartford Wolf Pack. Connecticut hockey fans now cheer for either the Pack or the Bridgeport Sound Tigers, also of the AHL.

Connecticut is looking toward the future by taking care of the environment. The state belongs to the Northeast Organic Farming Association, a nonprofit organization that is working to develop earth-friendly farming and gardening practices. The Connecticut Fund for the Environment, another nonprofit group, works to achieve better air and water quality in the state.

Great things come in small packages. That is true about Connecticut, one of the oldest states in the country. Residents and visitors can hike the state's mountains, relax on the beaches, or visit the museums. They can travel back to Pequot Indian, colonial, or prehistoric times, and people can enjoy vibrant cities and rural landscapes. As its residents know, Connecticut is a special state that offers something for everyone.

YEAR

1998    The Connecticut River becomes part of a program created to restore historically important waterways.

EVENT

- 31 -

# BIBLIOGRAPHY

Ciovacco, Justine, Kathleen A. Feeley, and Kristen Behrens. *State-by-State Atlas*. New York: DK Publishing, 2003.

Gutman, Bill. *The Look-It-Up Book of the 50 States*. New York: Random House, 2002.

King, David C. *Children's Encyclopedia of American History*. New York: DK Publishing, 2003.

Mead, Robin, Polly Mead, and Gary A. Lewis. *The Fifty States*. New York: Smithmark, 1992.

National Park Service, U.S. Department of the Interior. "Experience Your America: Connecticut." http://www.nps.gov/state/ct/.

Young, Donald, and Cynthia Overbeck Bix. *Our National Parks*. San Francisco: Sierra Club Books, 1990.

# INDEX